HOW TO DIE

Other Books By The Author

*The Future of Democracy:
Lessons from the Past and Present to
Guide Us on Our Path Forward*

The Death of Democracy

Truth & Democracy

Everyday Spirituality for Everyone

Guide to Living in a Democracy

The Pursuit of Happiness

What LOVE Does

HOW TO DIE

Embracing The Aging Process

by

Steve Zolno

REGENT PRESS
Berkeley, California
2025

Copyright © 2025 by Steve Zolno

paperback:
ISBN 13: 978-1-58790-713-5
ISBN 10: 1-58790-713-5

e-book:
ISBN 13: 978-1-58790-714-2
ISBN: 10: 1-58790-714-3

Library of Congress Control Number: 2025937335

Manufactured in the U.S.A.
Regent Press
Berkeley, California
www.regentpress.net
regentpress@mindspring.com

*To the many teachers I have had in my life,
and to people I encounter every day who share
their insights and wisdom.*

Contents

Preface 1

Introduction 5

The History of Death 11

A Sense Of Purpose 21

The Personal 27

The Interpersonal 35

The Political 43

The Past Is Present 49

The Future Is Present 57

Rites Of Passage 63

Exceeding Ourselves 71

Living and Dying Well 79

The Nature of Freedom 87

The Best Years Of Our Lives 95

The Final Transition 101

Preface

Janus is the Roman god of transitions. He looks back at the past and forward to the future at the same time. The month of January, that marks the transition from one year to the next, is named after him.

For the Romans, Janus represented moving from one phase of life to another. We each are constantly in transition; one moment yields to the next. In this moment what we consider the past is behind us and the future is yet to be lived.

Life's transitions are imperceptible as we go through them. Only when we look back do we believe that past events have taken place. Reality is a continuum and our ideas about the past and future are how we divide what we know into units that we can comprehend. Both as individuals and societies we continually create concepts, particularly about our history, to provide guidance for the future. But our concepts only are shallow representations of the real, continuous world.

If there is any "message" I hope to convey in this book, it is that who we really are and the real nature of the world lies outside our concepts. Why is this important and why even bother to state it?

For our entire lives we are trapped in a reality of our own making. This began when we were children and has continued to deepen for each of us during our time on Earth. But "once upon a time," as they say, we lived in a magical world where nothing was set, and then we became more certain about our ideas as we grew. Slowly the magic went away as we entered the world of our concepts and left our original one behind. Since then we have known that something is missing, but have been uncertain about what that is and how to return to it.

What is missing is that we have – for the most part – stopped seeing and replaced our direct experience with our ideas. We deprive ourselves of full participation in our encounters. But as we become aware of that, we can – if we choose – begin to understand how we mask reality and keep ourselves from its direct experience. If

PREFACE

we really pay attention we can begin to return to our lost magical world while retaining our conceptual guideposts.

What follows is an exploration of how and why we came to function as we do, and how to infuse our everyday experience with the enthusiasm we have lost. In a way this requires the death of the person we have created in our minds that many of us believe ourselves to be.

Regardless of whether we are aware of the process, we march inexorably along through the stages of our lives. We only have control over whether that procession will be as rewarding, upon taking our final breath, as we will have wanted it to be.

HOW TO DIE

Introduction

We begin to die from the moment we are born. But how we choose to live during our brief sojourn on Earth determines the quality of our time while here.

Life begins as an adventure of exploring and learning. We come in with a sense of energy and enthusiasm. But as we learn the ways of the world, our feeling of excitement begins to fade. We are told by our parents and others what to do and what to believe. As we get into a pattern of school, relationships, and work, we gradually assume an identity that limits our imagination and creativity.

We are dying – and being renewed – every moment of what we call life. New cells replace old cells – and new views replace old views – but this happens more slowly over time as we and our bodies become more stable and set in our ways. Some of us move quickly and recklessly toward our ultimate destination, while others are better at imparting a spirit of grace into our everyday experience.

The quality of our lives depends much more on what we bring to them than on what they bring to us. If we see our circumstances as overwhelming it will diminish our experience. If we maintain an openness to learning about others and the world, it will bring us a continually renewed sense of adventure.

Those who enjoy their lives the most maintain a sense of purpose. And what is that purpose? We begin unafraid to take on challenges and risks. Then we learn to proceed with caution, which gets in the way of a full life experience. Throughout our lives we hope to reconnect with the life force with which we came in and bring that into our daily interactions.

We once sought to expand our horizons, then our world began to shrink. We first were open to learning about others and the world, then began to believe we knew about them and forced them into the categories we forged. We paid less attention and stopped really seeing who and what was in front of us. Our vision narrowed to enable our participation in everyday functioning rather than expanding to accommodate the real world.

If we choose we can reaffirm our sense of purpose and again experience life more fully. We can train ourselves to no longer dwell on our limitations and that of our world; to focus once more on what is possible. As we do this our fear of death diminishes because we have a renewed sense of fulfillment.[1]

Introduction

Since death – and fear of death – is a dominant theme in the lives of most of us, we will devote much of the space in this book to addressing that issue.[2] But replacing that emphasis with a renewed interest in life is our real intention.

People – and many animals – spend much of their lives doing what they can to avoid death. But only we are able to contemplate life's end. Our fear of our ultimate destination dominates much of our time on earth. Some believe that an essential part of us goes on after we die, and some think that the death of the body is the end. There is no way to be certain about what death brings. No one really knows if there is a part of us that continues after the demise of the body.

Even though there is some consistency about reports from those who have been declared clinically dead that they see relatives and a "light at the end of the tunnel," those individuals actually went through near-death experiences and not death itself.[3, 4] There are those who report "out of body" experiences, but even if real, they don't tell us whether the part that left the body continues after its demise.

Death rituals and mourning have been part of human society as long as there have been people on earth. According to recent findings it also was a factor for some species that preceded us.[5] Yet when fear of death – and fear in general – dominate our lives we already are partly dead.

Much of our inhibition to leading full lives is based on concern about what others think. We largely form our ideas of what is right and wrong from the values of our culture, and act based on them. But we also are individuals with a capacity for experiencing and expressing unique perspectives in a joyful manner that most of us have forgotten.

When we allow our natural propensity to enjoy life to be experienced and expressed, we no longer are dependent on others or the world for fulfillment. Death no longer hovers over us when we have a profound appreciation for all that life brings.

At age five I was watching a television show with my family that dealt with death. The idea that life has an end struck me for the first time. I blurted out: "I don't want to die," and remained inconsolable for a long time despite the efforts of my mother to comfort me. She did her best to explain that we all die one day, and in my case that moment was a long way off.

It has taken me many years to understand that in our inevitable journey that begins at birth, our only real choice is how we experience our lives. After a lifetime of soul-searching – and a search for the existence of a soul – it has become clear to me that a major part of living at its fullest includes a willingness to embrace all it brings, including its end, and that this view enhances our experience for its duration.

Our time on earth is brief. Some of us embrace all – or most of – what comes our way and some live in denial of their connectedness to others and the world around them. We share an identical ultimate destiny, but some make their time here a living hell – even while aware of what awaits them – while others experience a greater amount of fulfillment in their everyday encounters.

Each moment yields to yet another, and for most of it we have little control. We usually can't predict whether our daily interactions will lead to fulfillment or regret. All of us experience times of pain and disappointment, as well as moments of joy and elation. All we really can do is witness what appears on our plate as the years advance. But it is what we do with what occurs in the course of our daily lives that makes the difference, not only in the end, but in every ongoing moment.

For some of us the number of days is more limited than for others. But it seems to me that a short life enjoyed is preferable to a long one filled with fear and resentment. No matter how hard we pursue our goals it is not worldly success that brings satisfaction, but our ability and willingness to fully experience what we encounter.

With each passing moment we make choices that affect the quality of our lives. When I project disappointment upon what I experience – and thus on my mind – I already am defeated; when I choose to engage openly – rather than simply reacting – I live a life of constructive dialogue with the world, those around me, and myself. This little book is a meditation on how, despite life's daily surprises, what we bring to our experience, more than the experience itself, determines the quality of our brief time on Earth.

In these pages we discuss how our lives have become less meaningful with what we call "maturity," and how we can restore the sense of wonder we left behind. But words cannot force people to take on a view that renews their joy in life. Only when we identify and restore the enthusiasm we once knew does a dynamic involvement once again come into play. While fully engaged with others and the world, and focusing on the enjoyment of each moment rather than our demise, we overcome the fear of death in our daily lives.

*Earth's story is the saga of differentiation –
of the separation and concentration of elements
into new rocks and minerals, into continents and
seas, and ultimately into life.*

– ROBERT M. HAZEN[6]

The History of Death

To understand the present we must go back to the roots of the human race as best we can. That then leads us further to the origins of life. And that takes us to the beginning of the known universe and of time's continuum.

The belief of modern science – and many religions – is that everything started with a sudden act of creation or "Big Bang." Since that beginning there has been a continuous flow of events – which also can be seen as one event – that has progressed right up to and through the present.

Thus each of us and all that surrounds us are part of the ongoing march of time. We are participants in the momentum of evolution

– including the creation of our universe, solar system, the Earth, and terrestrial life – that began in time immemorial and continually moves forward.

From the beginning of time as we know it there has been a slow transformation of the universe; a gradual ongoing process that led to the present and continues through it. There have been great upheavals including earthquakes and volcanic eruptions, but these were the result of a slow buildup of forces within the earth that ultimately resulted in cataclysmic change.

It has been stated that history is "just one damn thing after another." Perhaps the same can be said about time. But time is a continuum we break into segments for our convenience to enable us to describe events. We must do this to discuss our history and that of our universe. But our descriptions of the progression of time are snapshots of representational moments; they provide only a sketch of the real flow of events. Thus our perceptions – and understanding – are limited.

Different historians (and those scientists we might call prehistorians) emphasize different moments of the past just as individuals provide varying versions of the same event. We only can describe bits of what we want to convey, and then string them together into a cohesive story as best we can. Time unfolds continuously, yet our words and sentences – and even our scientific formulas that seem so comprehensive – only can provide a limited reflection of what actually happens.

The beginning of our universe, and everything that followed including the present and beyond, is one ongoing event, but we divide it into time periods to aid our understanding. We also divide the world – and the people in it – into categories for our convenience. Those divisions don't exist in nature; they only are our creation.

Going back to the earliest beginnings we know of, scientists believe that our universe was thrust into existence about 14 billion years ago, and that matter soon formed from the energy that resulted, creating the stars, sun and eventually our planet. Evidence points to a continually expanding universe, thus the belief it had a beginning. Countless solar systems resulted from the cosmic dust that slowly coalesced into celestial bodies, while many still are being created and destroyed.[7]

The Earth spun off from the sun about 4.5 billion years ago. Evidence points to the likelihood that our planet started as a fiery ball that turned to rock as it cooled. Water is believed to have appeared near the beginning, and eventually to have shaped much of the earth's features by slowly wearing away the basaltic crust.[8]

Let's take a tour of the primeval sludge that made up Earth's surface of perhaps four billion years ago when life is believed to have begun. According to the story recorded in rocks – as interpreted by earth scientists – there were no continents as we now know them. Land masses eventually appeared – and then disappeared – over millions of years as magma (lava) rose from openings in the planet's crust. Because of the unpredictability of Earth's early changes it is doubtful that anyone witnessing its progression would have been able to predict the shape of things to come.

The surface of the earth cooled for about a billion years and then, in the recesses of the sludge, there lurked the first representations of life. These single-celled beginnings – while gradually gaining in complexity – continued to develop for eons. Actual multi-celled "creatures" that could swim – or eventually walk – were roughly three billion years away.

We don't know what put the "spark" into life. We only can guess at the process that led to its origins, as our scientists never have been able to re-create it. There still is much controversy about the interpretation of the record told by rocks. But essentially, about four billion years ago, simple cells began to use oxygen to reproduce, without much change beyond that for perhaps three billion years. Once reproduction became possible it signaled the beginning of life as we know it.

What followed is fairly well agreed upon by biologists. Multi-cellular life began about one billion years ago. Plants became gradually more complex, and then the simplest animals appeared in the sea or warm ponds about 540 million years ago. Animals diversified based on mutations that were selected as advantageous by their environment. One hypothetical example of how animals may have moved onto land: if primitive swimming animals developed leg-like appendages over countless generations, this would have enabled those creatures to function on land and water. The ability of these – our ancestors – to move back and forth between water and land, and eventually to dwell permanently on land from a gradually disappearing tide pool or lake, would have enhanced their chances of survival.

During the slow and incremental development of life into gradually more complex forms, when did individual creatures begin to recognize their existence? Did the most basic animals choose their meals or mates, or did instinct and habit guide every move? And are we describing "choice" when we discuss the behavior of creatures that might barely be recognizable as animals to our current perceptions, let alone appearing human?

Our first upright ancestors in the fossil record of those considered anatomical humans – Homo Habilis – lived in South and East Africa about two million years ago. Two million years seems long by our standards, but it only is five one-hundredths of a percent, or .0005, of the entire time of the existence of life on earth.

The fossil record shows that the bodies and brain cavities of our ancestors increased in size, which means that thinking and planning – and possibly an increasing ability to coordinate their efforts with others – improved their chances of survival. Again we might ask if this is when choice can be said to have begun. Was it the choice of our human ancestors to work with others for the common good that contributed to the continuation of their species?[9]

Pre-humans continued to advance in complexity and in their ability to master their changing environments. They gradually adapted more successfully to their world in comparison with their predecessors. Meanwhile species that could not adapt to environmental changes – the vast majority – became extinct.

At some point – or, more likely, over a long period of time – there came a change in consciousness that led them – and eventually us – to become fully human. From then on they began to think of themselves as beings with a past and future and with a separate existence from their surroundings. They eventually developed the ability to know – or think they know – who they are as individuals in addition to being members of a group or society. They established a self-concept and created names for themselves. But only with the idea of a self – with a beginning and end – did the idea of death become possible. Recent research reveals that one of the species that preceded us – homo neladi – buried their dead in a ritualistic fashion about 300,000 years ago.[10]

When our ancestors recognized themselves as distinct beings with a history spanning birth to death, as well as being part of a society with ancient roots, they began to envision a future for which they tried to prepare themselves and their children. Planning by small groups involving food storage, for example, eventually resulted in societies that sought to guarantee their future by maintaining quantities of grain to withstand drought and other natural disasters.

With the advent of language early societies developed stories about themselves and their communities. They gained an interest and ability to remember and know the myths that were their earliest idea of history, first by oral tradition and later in written form. They began to plan for the days and years ahead. They honored births; they recognized and feared death and created rituals to commemorate those they lost.[11] They developed knowledge of ways to act to increase their chances of survival – moral codes – based on stories of ancestors, as reflected in myths such as those of the ancient Greeks and stories found in the Bible.

At some point human beings living in groups decided there is a division between "us" and "them" – those who are like us and those who are not; those we trust or do not; those with whom we choose to cooperate or compete; those who are human in the same way we are and those who are not. Our identity – our idea of "self" – included our concept of membership in a society, race, religion, gender, or any other group that became an essential part of how we think of ourselves. Our lives – and deaths – became part of our story. And to this day, our identity cannot be separated from the group labels we place upon ourselves and others.

When we say we were "born," we consider ourselves to be an addition to the group or groups of which we think ourselves to be part. And we describe death as a departure of someone who belonged to specific groups – for example, a white Christian male who was a member of the group of bankers and golfers, or part of the group who contributed time and money to organizations to help relieve poverty.

At times we wonder if we are an entity beyond the groups of which we see ourselves as members. Is there anything essential to our basic identity that is not part of a group? And beyond our body is there an essential self? Does this self appear with the advent of the body and then disappear with its destruction? These are questions that undoubtedly have been asked for millennia.

The "self" most of us believe to be our identity is a body we see as separate from everything around us. But that "self" actually is a creation we hold in our minds that allows us to function as individuals. Just like every other entity in nature, our bodies come into being by combining the elements that exist in every living thing for a limited time, and then dissipate into the infinite cacophony we call space.

Thus the reality of who we are is a continuum that goes back to the origin of the universe and will continue for as long as time persists. The gradual advent of life as we know it reaches from our origins as a part of the entirety of existence through the present, cascading inexorably into an unknown future. From the view of the whole, we are a barely perceptible but essential part of that process.

We all seek a cause beyond ourselves...we all require devotion to something more than ourselves for our lives to be endurable.

– Atul Gawande[12]

A Sense of Purpose

In their final hours, perhaps the most common sentiment expressed by those who know they are dying is regret: "If only I had lived my life with a greater sense of purpose." "If only I had been more forgiving."[13, 14] They also often ask forgiveness from others for not having been more loving.

Is it possible to live so we can be the person that our dying self would want us to be? Can we act in the present so we don't regret not having been the person we believe we should be?

We start out in life being open and loving to everyone around us. We express ourselves spontaneously and creatively throughout our childhood. Then we learn to think we are limited beings and begin to consider ourselves separate from everything and everyone. Our lives become governed by that view of separateness. We act from the confines of the self-image we have adopted and interact cautiously lest we get hurt.

We are taught that success is based on getting ahead of others. We begin to believe that competition and accumulation are the routes to happiness.

We started in a mode of discovery and adventure and continue to hold that ideal in our minds. We are expected to live by the values of our society that we are taught. But a memory of that original spark remains with us, so we often regret how we have lived our lives.

Undoubtedly there are dangers against which we must defend ourselves – from others and even from nature. But we can retreat into a view that we always must be on guard, where we see people as a physical danger or a threat to our success and self-esteem. And they may see us the same way.

Our patterns of seeing the world are established early. We habitually blame a person, group, or the circumstances of our lives for our negative feelings and find it nearly impossible to give up that blame as it seems to be a part of who we are. Our blame and prejudices become essential to our identity.[15]

Although we have developed habits of relating to the world based on what we have learned or what we are told, we never are forced to act out of a sense of alienation or disconnection. Rather, we can choose at any moment, including this one, to act based on an understanding of the common humanity that connects us with others.

That sentiment often comes gushing forth when we realize there is little time left to us. But we can know now – and for as long as we are on this planet – that we not only retain within us that sense of purpose of connecting with others and the world, but can reclaim it at any time. To do this we must go beyond it as a concept: it is tied to a feeling that supersedes our idea about who we are and how we should interact. It is that natural sense of connection with which we began and to which we long to return.[16] But that involves sacrificing some of the cherished identity we have developed.

Throughout our lives we miss our original openness. We hope that others or circumstances will restore it to us. But our connection to all that is around us cannot be restored because it always has been our condition and never has been diminished except in our minds. If we choose we can acknowledge and act from that understanding. Following through on that insight can change our lives, those of others, and possibly the world. That perspective has the potential to affect all of our actions, including the personal, the interpersonal and the political.

If we always think of the feeling we want as a goal for the future, it perpetually will elude us. But if we allow ourselves to feel that connection in the present, which is the only time we can do anything, we immediately experience our sense of purpose.

In any moment we can remind ourselves about that view and change our actions to express it. But doing this takes a clear vision and a great deal of courage. It seems that everyone around us is acting from a sense of preservation of their separate selves. But once we open to people – to really hearing the plea beneath what they seem to be wanting – we can see they actually desire the same thing we are seeking: a genuine and feeling connection with others; a belief in their own validity; recognition for the person they really are beneath the façade of separateness.

Although the spirit is willing, as they say, what stands in the way of truly opening ourselves to others and the world is fear of losing our carefully constructed sense of being a separate self. Allowing a deep connection with another seems to threaten our existence.

It is one thing to look back and state regrets. It is another to clarify how to act in a way that

A Sense of Purpose

is expressive of our real self. You might ask what you imagine you think you would regret not having done in your life and how you could make that happen in the present and perhaps for its remainder.

You might consider how you can express appreciation for your essential nature and that of others. In what ways are you – or those you encounter – unique? Do you – or they – have a view of life you can share? How could you begin opening up to that? How could we each be more gracious and sharing of ourselves with everyone we meet?

There are other ways to express our inner or true self. We might imagine how we can be creative in a way that would allow us to share more of ourselves with people. We each have skills that have not fully been developed. We also might consider how we can encourage others to develop their talents; when we do this we become more in touch with our own creative abilities.

There are those who habitually express the vision they have adopted of the world as being that of hatred and divisiveness. This is what life has taught them. But rather than getting caught in their cynicism, we can continue to promote our true nature of connectedness which leads to compassion, and perhaps that will kindle the same perspective in them. Many seem to have given up on that view, as it is rarely expressed between people in our society. But we don't need the permission of others to express our real selves.

Within each of us there two world views that are reflected in all we do. One is that of connectedness. The other is one of disconnection. One mode is born of being in the present, the other comes from anticipation and fear of others or the future.

When we feel connected we are optimistic we can work with others toward common solutions to our issues, but when we feel disconnected we assume that solutions are unlikely and we adopt a position of defensiveness during which we prepare ourselves to compete or even go to war.

If we continually dwell on how awful the world is, we always will feel awful. Despite our efforts to control our lives, we don't know what the future will bring. But we can allow ourselves to appreciate what we are given in each moment: perhaps a sunset or a sunrise, or rain and clouds, or the people with whom we interact. That is how we bring ourselves the experience we seek.

Our purpose is accomplished by allowing ourselves to experience our connection with others and the world. We then can choose to follow wherever that may lead.

The hero is ... an aspect of human nature, the aspect that hears the call from the deeper self and answers it.

– Paul Rebillot[18]

The Personal

Humans have three essential needs: the sustenance of the body, the stimulation of the mind, and the recognition of the soul.

The body needs no introduction, although our understanding of it always falls short. The image we hold in our minds of our body – and that of others – never is accurate because the body is more complex than we can comprehend. It has layers of interwoven systems that are continually in flux. For our convenience we give it a name as we fail to notice that the body of an adult has little or no resemblance to the child who preceded it. About 98% of our atoms change yearly, while some of the atoms of which we are made once were a part of the bodies of others and all that surrounds us, and then we regularly return them to our surroundings.[19]

What we call the mind is the neurological part of the body. Our life experience is held in that system, which culminates in the brain. It is where our perceptions, memories and projections onto the world are held. What we know – or think we know – is processed there.[20]

Our minds are the thoughts and reactions through which we filter and interpret what is brought to us by our perceptions. They contain our ideas about how others and the world work. Once they are established, we usually prefer to retain our theories despite changes that may occur around us. That would force us to "change our minds," but we usually would rather cling to what we think we know. The rigidity of our thoughts – and our actions based on them – allows us to be consistent, but fails to fit the ever-changing world around us. Our ideas about people – and ourselves – only permit us to see a reflection of who they really are. Our labels fail to acknowledge many aspects of people including the feeling side of who they are.

Although scientists consider the brain to be the seat of the mind, and many experiments have been done based on that view, there is another part of us not amenable to physical verification.

That is what some call our essence or "soul." It has been our most essential identity since birth. It witnesses our bodies and thoughts as well as our actions based on them. It is the part of you that – in this moment – observes that you are reading what is on this page and also witnesses you reacting to what you read. It is the part that always has been – and always will be – the real "you," although you may think you are your body or the thoughts that surge through it.

We see ourselves as individuals who are buffeted about by the circumstances of our lives. When things go well according to our expectations we tend to feel well. When things go poorly we tend to feel poorly.

But our feelings have little to do with the actual circumstances of our lives and much to do with our expectations for how we and the world should be and how others should treat us. From the beginning we have a built-in expectation of nurturance from our mothers, and we cry, often at the top of our lungs, when that expectation is not met. When eventually we find that crying no longer gets us what we want, we learn to whine and complain to our parents until they (hopefully) give in, much as my parents did.

And then for the rest of our lives we continue that pattern as we habitually complain about others, the world, and their shortcomings. But as we complain we rarely see that we hurt ourselves by creating a negative frame of mind – including a state of physical tension – even when our complaints lead to very little change.

Throughout our lives we witness an endless stream of events that vary from what we consider the positive to the negative – often many times in one day. But our experience reflects our reactions rather than the events themselves. Our judgments are built into all we see; people, places, and even everyday objects are seen as good or bad. Examples include our views of politics and competitive situations where the winners feel good and the losers experience disappointment. Thus the mind imposes its own interpretation on events that can lead us to extremes in our moods in a short period of time. Even the anticipation of events – or a fantasy about them – can catapult us into positive or negative mood swings.[21]

Our reaction to many events also depends on our idea of how they affect – or will affect – our self-esteem. If we see ourselves as winners, we experience relaxation and an expanding breath. Blood flows to our heart at an increased rate. We have an experience similar to what it is like to be loved. If we see ourselves as losers, we experience tension and our breath becomes shallow. Our heart rate contracts and we may think of ourselves as unlovable.

When things seem to go well we feel well, at least temporarily, and cling to what feels like a positive mental state, trying to maintain or repeat what we thought got us to that place. When things appear to go poorly, we usually hope for an improvement in circumstances, which would translate into an improved mental state.

But the mind also has a "mind" of its own. At times our moods fluctuate for no reason we can decipher, or we become stuck in a down place from which there seems to be no exit. At such times a change in our environment appears to have no effect.

Knowledge and understanding are motivating factors we use to guide our actions. Success in the hunt once was based on our knowledge of the hunted, and success in the modern world also is based on the accuracy of the model we hold in our minds.[22]

Once they have been established, we cling to our views of ourselves, others and the world, and remain on guard against anyone or anything we see threatening them. They become part of our identity and we fear losing them much as we fear death itself.

In our minds we fluctuate between a positive and negative view of ourselves and others. But our judgments often have more to do with the ever-changing moods of our minds than anything imposed by our surroundings.

As we age, we usually become more set in our views and ways. We become more rigid and less flexible, forcing reality into our preset notions. We pay less attention to our surroundings as we believe our long experience has taught us the essentials of what we need to know.[23]

Over time we become guided more by our views than what the world brings us – more by our concepts than reality itself. We are less viable and truly alive; more a self-contained reality than a dynamic presence connecting with the world.

But there is an alternative. As we interact with others and the world we can begin to open ourselves to the possibility that what we think we know may fall short. We can rely less on our concepts than on what our experience brings us. We can open ourselves to the possibility that our interactions once again can be joyous as they were in our earliest youth. And it is to that realization that many come in their final years or even on their deathbed. The old Scrooge within can yield to the younger version if we simply realize that the current version fails to serve us in getting what we most want, which is emotional interaction with the world.

Then it becomes clear we have a choice. We can allow ourselves a full experience of the ups and downs to which we always will be subject. And as we become willing participants in the unpredictable drama of our lives – whatever direction they take – we become less victims of each wave and more willing riders on each crest as it approaches and leads to the next.

HOW TO DIE

Precursors of wisdom, such as empathy, emotional regulation, and critical thinking, can be modeled and explicitly taught from an early age.

– Daniel Levitin[24]

The Interpersonal

When we start out in life we have no preset ideas about others.[25] We engage in interactions enthusiastically and energetically. We encounter people with our entire being. But the nurturance we desire from others – both materially and emotionally – becomes a major need we actively seek.

While still young we discard our direct perception of people for concepts of them, often based on whether they meet our needs. We begin to see them more through our filters than the naïve perceptions we once used. This begins with our parents then moves out to family, friends and others.

Our self-concept is based largely on the positive or negative feedback we receive. Our identity forms around how others react to us and what they tell us about ourselves. They convey whether or not we are worthwhile human beings deserving of love.

But no matter how much others assure us – including parents, friends, teachers, partners, spouses, and work associates – no one can make us secure in our self-esteem. We remain vulnerable to what others think of us throughout our lives. Positive feedback allows us to feel good about ourselves and negative feedback often puts us into a funk.

If we are stuck in a negative self-image, positive feedback will simply slide off. Yet we continue to seek praise to fill in a hole that dwells deep within. Those rare individuals who are able to maintain a positive self-image do not as often rely on others to give them a sense of confidence.

We have acquired a habit of waiting for people to nurture and love us enough to make our lives fulfilling, but it seems there never is enough nurturance to satisfy us for long. So our self-esteem varies from one person and situation to another as we do what we can to get the emotional support we seek.

Our psychological and emotional dependence on others lies just beneath the surface. The identity we form and present to the world of being independent of how people see and treat us persists throughout our lives.

We develop a positive façade so that others don't suspect our vulnerability. We don't want people to know that what they think affects us deeply, so we act as if we don't care. But inside we look to the next interaction to boost our self-image.

It is a return to our original sense of connection with others we seek. But we also can recognize that no one – and no event – can restore what we left behind. That is because that connection never really went away. If we choose we can begin to interact with others from that viewpoint. That way of being can become omnipresent in our daily interactions.

But how does that look in the real world?

The sense of separateness we create between ourselves and others leaves us feeling isolated. But we actually have manufactured those barriers in our minds. The alternative is first acknowledging the connection that already is there. This can be done within ourselves without even saying a word.

Instead of waiting for others to connect with us, we can recognize our common humanity. If we are hoping for the other to do this it may never happen. We don't need to reach out to initiate our connection; it already is established. Opportunities to act from this reality present themselves constantly. There is no one right or wrong way to express it, but everyday occasions provide opportunities to convey what already exists.

Just as we want others to acknowledge the real self behind our image, they want that from us. This requires acknowledging the inner being of those with whom we interact. As we do that the words and gestures flow naturally.

What if some people seem difficult and we prefer to avoid them altogether? We can keep in mind that feeling disconnected from those we encounter creates a barrier that also affects us negatively. Patience may be required before we can begin to alter our interactions. Sometimes the communication style of others requires feedback about how it affects us, but this can be done while maintaining our sense of connection and without condemnation.

Once we establish that in our minds, we can be creative in how it's experienced and expressed. It may assume a spontaneous form beyond that to which we are accustomed.

When we relate from total respect for others we merge our minds in a very real way and create a whole new entity. There is a sense of trust where neither feels a need to dominate. But this requires that we go beyond our preconceptions of others as we want them to move beyond their preconceptions of us.

We often would rather maintain our ideas about people than view them anew in each moment. But when our minds and hearts are open, our perceptions of each other continue to change.

Of course there are those who prove unworthy of our trust even after opening a dialogue to communicate about issues, or giving them a series of chances to prove they are trustworthy. At that point we may need to cut off our contact, which hopefully can be repaired, but it also is essential to protect ourselves when necessary.

If we really watch we begin to see that everything in our world – including those in it – is continually in flux. We usually think of other people – and ourselves – as static forms rather than acknowledging their ever-changing nature. This is how our minds enable us to function easily in our interactions. The advantage is that we don't need to continually observe others to get to know them. The disadvantage is that our limited images become irrelevant to the changing nature of people.

When in touch with the ongoing reality of others, our minds remain flexible and hone closer to the truth. When open to people and the world as we find them – rather than as we conceive them – it establishes a state of connection where we are relaxed and our hearts receptive.

Beyond that, when really paying attention, we begin seeing the potential for good in others. That comes from recognizing their true nature, which is beyond our concepts, and providing them the forgiveness we want for ourselves.

We are made of an infinite number of components, including our physical appearance, our views of the world, our talents and skills, and the complex systems that make up our bodies. We know little about others except what we experience, and that only gives us a hint of the larger whole.

Thus to best get to know people, we need to be willing to acknowledge how little we actually do know and open ourselves to seeing layers that may have been hidden. This only can be done on an ongoing basis as more eventually is revealed.

We frequently are unwilling to give up our assumptions about others for fear of losing a part of ourselves – the part that thinks it understands them and the world. All we know is what we experience within ourselves. The more openly we observe people, the more we see how much we have in common .

Getting to know people beyond our words and descriptions provides a much more accurate picture of who they are. When open to what others evoke in us beyond the concept we hold in our minds, the idea of ourselves to which we cling begins to dissolve and – in a very real way – we become the other.

In each moment we can ask ourselves if we are acting as lovingly as we can. Rather than expecting the love and support we want, we can provide it to those around us. This is how we best bring the experience we seek to ourselves.

HOW TO DIE

*A man who cannot live in society, or who
has no need to do so because he is self-sufficient,
is either a beast or a god.*

– Aristotle[26]

The Political

As our earliest ancestors joined groups to enhance their chances of survival, a way to govern their members was needed. They had to make crucial decisions about areas such as where to hunt, and also create rules about how to interact with each other.

As groups enlarged from band to tribe to state to nation, there was greater stability, but individuals and small groups no longer could make rules – and then laws – that affected them, as that became the role of the state. But rules and laws often came at the cost of suppressing individual freedom. Thus a major issue always has been how to make and enforce laws that best help societies function.

Throughout history the most prevalent political entity has been autocracy, which is rule by one leader or representatives of that leader. Democracy, from the ancient Greek, meaning "rule by the people," has been rare and usually of relatively short duration.

The ultimate aim of any social organization – from a small group to a large nation – is to provide stability for its members. Because people often feel that their needs are neglected, there have been rebellions too numerous to count. When stability is established at the cost of personal freedom it often inspires rebellion among those who consider themselves oppressed.

Laws in autocracies generally are made to benefit those in power. Taxation and other laws that were seen primarily to benefit the English monarchy inspired the American colonies to rebel.

As part of our membership in a state (or nation or country) we take on a group identity. Our idea of who we are includes those groups. We become a Russian, an American or Spaniard, which improves our sense of security. Loyalty to a leader or country – or "patriotism" – is an important element of the identity for most people. According to Hobbes, any state is preferable to none because of the stability it provides.[27]

So how do we find a balance between the needs of the individual and the efficiency of the state? Our attempt to explore that leads us to consider the differences between autocracy and democracy.

There is a desire for freedom inherent in humanity. But putting aside our individual needs to accommodate what is best for the group or country also seems to be a genetic trait: our identity gets absorbed into a larger entity for what is seen as the greater good. This has affected our actions from the time of the earliest bands of hunters to the establishment of our modern states.

We sacrifice our identity or "die" as individuals to ensure the viability of an organism – the state – that is greater than ourselves. This impulse – which also exists in many animals – makes us become absorbed into groups, flocks and packs.

A 2000 year gap exists from the time of the ancient Greek democracy and Roman Republic to the founding of the United States by democratic principles, although democracy is mentioned nowhere in its Constitution. Like all rebellions before and since, the US Revolution was fought in opposition to what the rebels considered an infringement of their freedoms. There have been countless revolutions; most have failed.

Even after a regime seen as oppressive is overturned, a democratic system rarely replaces it. Knowing we don't want oppression is common; knowing what we want to put in its place – and an ability to accomplish that – is a much greater challenge.

Based on their experience with centralized authority, the American founders created a loose association under the Articles of Confederation that did not require the colonies to act as one nation, but allowed individual governance, much as if they were thirteen separate nations. This situation failed to work, so after ten years those founders who were available collaborated to write a more forward looking Constitution that created a centralized government.

Throughout the history of the United States there has been a continual debate about whether government by "We The People" means that the needs and views of all should be taken into account or only those of some. But if the idea of "We The People" is to be taken seriously by those who write the laws – and everyday Americans – we cannot leave out anyone based on religion, race, background, identity, or even beliefs they hold.

So how do we include those who think their needs should take priority over the general good? How do we return to the sense of common purpose with which every revolution began?

At times of crisis what unites us is an effort to

defeat a common enemy, whether it be another nation, a natural disaster or a financial meltdown. Those situations bring out the best in us because they enable us to participate in a cause where all are equal in their devotion to overcoming an obstacle to their freedom or wellbeing.[28]

People want to be acknowledged by others and their government. They want a system that responds to their needs. For some, that means that government protects them or supports them in getting their needs met. For others, that may simply mean leaving them alone, as long as they are not violating the rights of others.

In democracies laws are based on the idea that people and their needs are similar. They seek opportunities to pursue their dreams in peace and avoid the aggressions of others. That understanding contributes to the "common law"[29] that largely governs us. Most laws are based on a history of human aggression, rather than on our compassion or connectedness. There is little need to govern the latter.

Thus laws are about avoiding a repeat of negative behaviors while they fail to describe the positive. In our legal systems our common humanity – including our will to look after each other – is overlooked for an emphasis on the negative side of human nature. So it is up to each of us, in our everyday interactions, as well as those who represent us in our governments, to think about how best to emphasize our common needs rather than the competitiveness that leads to some people having an advantage over others.

We can emphasize solutions rather than problems. We can act from an understanding that when we make our world a better place for others we also do that for ourselves, our children and those who follow us.

In this way we become part of a movement for the improvement of our world for generations to come, rather than its degradation. When our efforts contribute to a positive outcome for others and our planet, we mandate that our species will live on indefinitely into the future.

Let go of the past. Less is so much more.
– STREET ART IN SAN LUIS OBISPO, CA

The Past is Present

Our ideas about ourselves, others and the world, which we think of as representing the "true" nature of things, actually are based on selective memories.[30] Thus we create the world in which we live, and we each have a different view of reality established over the duration of our lives. But our thoughts about the past take place in the present.

We are multi-faceted entities with innumerable qualities, as is everyone who inhabits our planet. The earth and universe are continually changing. But our descriptions and understanding are based on the past and refer to what has gone before. They cannot accurately describe the uniqueness of each moment.

If I use the word "tree" – even to describe an object in front of me – I refer to all my previous experience with objects I and others have labeled as trees. The term does not adequately describe what I actually am perceiving, which is different from all other objects I have seen.

We establish our self-concepts early in life and tend to believe ourselves limited to our ideas of who we are. Our concepts of ourselves are constructed of memories of how we have seen us acting in the past that includes our limits and potential.[31] To live as consistent individuals – which we consider the nature of sanity – we have learned to narrow our self-concepts to exclude any aspects that fall outside them.

Once we have established our ideas about our personalities, interests, talents, tastes, gender, race, and every other aspect we think of as "me," we are unlikely to change them. But we may work to move toward goals that fall within the idea we have of ourselves, for example, to expand our athletic or academic skills, or take on greater challenges in our areas of interest.

If we think of ourselves as being an angry person, our actions will reflect that self-image, and if we think of ourselves as calm, that idea will dominate our actions. Moving outside our comfort zone is difficult. If we are asked to change or go beyond our self-imposed limits, we will respond, or at least think: "That's the way I am."

Children live in a world of what we call

"play," where they quickly can change identities as do the objects they use as toys. But the many identities they easily take on are closer to the reality of human nature than the forced single personalities of adults.

Eventually, to function in the "real world," most children assume a consistent identity. But we all know at some level that who we profess to be only is the surface of a much more complex being. We seek recognition throughout our lives for who we really are, although we may not actually have a clear idea of our true nature.

Those who fail to play the role of a consistent individual – as we all do at times – find they are shunned by those around them who have learned to expect a single facade to which they can relate. Varying too greatly from the persona we have established brings us close to the border of insanity.

Trying to describe the setting you now are in will demonstrate how the nature of reality supersedes our descriptions. If you are indoors perhaps there are chairs, tables, lamps, couches, dressers, or curtains, among other objects; certainly there is a floor, walls and ceiling. Upon close observation we find each of those objects to be different from others we call by the same name, that is, most chairs are different than others, as are most tables, lamps, couches, etc.

If outdoors, there is an infinity of objects to observe, perhaps trees, grass, clouds, trails, pavement, or automobiles. And once more, on inspection, each of those objects has a unique set of characteristics not shared by the others we give the same name. But in our thoughts and descriptions we already have established similar objects as the same and fail to distinguish between them.

We also hold preset concepts of people in our minds. We try to understand those we encounter by putting then into categories of race, religion, sexual orientation, intelligence, age group and the lifestyle they seem to live, before we really know anything about them. When we do get to know people, we often stop really paying attention to the variances in personality they express.

Our concepts of others and the world rarely are able to move beyond our preset groupings. This makes us fail to objectively observe who and what we see and move toward a more realistic understanding. And if we are able to move beyond our preset categories, the words we use to describe people and objects will not be adequate because they are based in the past.

So how do we reach a real understanding of what we experience? And perhaps more importantly, how do we describe reality in a way that encompasses the truth of what is there rather than our preconceptions?

Comprehending the reality beyond what we have trained ourselves to see requires a genuine mental shift and courage to let go of how we have seen the world our entire lives. It requires a willingness to return to our original way of seeing with which most of us – at least at first – will find uncomfortable.

On the other hand, allowing ourselves to return to simply viewing the world and others outside the realm of the filters we normally impose is what sages throughout history have referred to as freeing of the mind, as in the famous quote from John I: "The truth shall set you free."

Simply paying attention to what we see – rather than imposing a veil of words and concepts as we traditionally have done – gives us new insight into the nature of reality. This is why scientists, philosophers, and writers, in pursuit of truth, often have rejected the descriptions of those who came before, while still building on those who preceded them.

What we are discussing is not only the realm of intellectuals or deep thinkers. Within every human being is a place that seeks truth. That's why we appreciate those who see us without judgement – usually our mothers and perhaps a few others – although we are willing to judge other people, the world and even ourselves based on our ideas for how they should be.

Our descriptions contain inherent judgments. Words create an ideal in our minds, but the reality they describe is beyond our words. Going back to "tree," we hold a mental ideal for what a tree is, but no tree in the real world comes up to that ideal. We also hold ideals for others and ourselves to which no one can aspire.

When we regret having been less than our ideal selves, such as making mistakes we later become aware of, or treating people unkindly, we can realize that the past, by definition, is behind us. Putting our time into contemplating what we should or could have done is a self-imposed exercise in futility. If we have learned from the past, it will be demonstrated by taking more thoughtful actions in the present. And the past we create in our minds only is a limited perspective on what actually happened.

So freedom is not an unattainable goal. It is realizing that the real world is different from the one of our ideals and releasing ourselves from the prison of our thoughts as we open ourselves to seeing what is in front of us.

How does this insight affect our actions? We can be aware that our descriptions always have differed, and will continue to differ, from reality, which we may never know. We use the words available to us to describe the world as best we can. And we understand that we no longer are certain that we ever can describe what is real. Humility is perhaps the most essential lesson.

Admitting the limits of our understanding frees us from the expectation that we ever will be able to fully describe what is true. We are forced to admit how little we know. But this causes us to bring more compassion toward ourselves and others as we become aware of our human limitations. This puts our mind at ease because we see others and ourselves more directly and clearly as we sacrifice the self of our perceptions for a more true self.

HOW TO DIE

> *"As Socrates so philosophically put it,
> since we don't know what death is,
> it is illogical to fear it."*
>
> – Guildenstern, in *Rosencrantz and
> Guildenstern are Dead* by Tom Stoppard

The Future Is Present

Our concepts of the future – including our fears and aspirations – are based on ideas we hold in our minds from the past.

Our true nature – with its infinite aspects – remains beyond our concepts. But our ideas about what we want for the future are based on what we believe to be the shortcomings of our current lives.

We want our future lives and selves to be different – and better – than our current situation, based on a perennial assumption that the present is not quite good enough. Desiring our future to be more financially secure assumes it is not secure enough now. Focusing on improved relationships means we believe our current ones are not quite up to our expectations. Looking forward to a vacation may mean we seek relief from our everyday existence.

We are chronically critical about the state of affairs that surround us. Our ideas for how our world should be are based on a memory of a better past that never really was, or hope for a future that is unlikely to come.

It is rare to allow ourselves to appreciate our current situation, including our lives, relationships and state of affairs. Our minds nearly always focus – intentionally or not – on our idea of how we want things to be. We often are critical of others, our political situation, and even ourselves. But our thoughts take place in the only time we can do anything, which is the present moment.

The ultimate fear many carry in their minds is how they will approach life's final stages. Will our twilight years bring us relief from the stress of everyday life? As we near the end will we be able to look back with no regrets, or will we wish we had lived differently? Is our end something to fear, or will we be content as we embark on our final journey?

You might consider an experiment to determine your degree of satisfaction in life. Try to describe what is happening in this moment. Can you do that and stay in the present? If you find yourself describing what happened in the recent or distant past you are not actually discussing the present.

When you attempt to describe the present with no reference to the past you will find it a difficult task. You may discover that the moment keeps changing with the passage of time and there are no words to adequately describe it.

When we stop thinking for a moment about our present experience we may find we only are left with feelings that our thoughts have masked. There always are emotions behind our thoughts, mostly about whether what we are contemplating is positive or negative. The positive feeling we hope to experience by our actions is what motivates us.

The ideals we hold for our lives – whether about relations, finance, or other goals – come with an assumption they will make us feel good. We pursue what we want with the hope that when we attain it the reward will be a feeling of satisfaction. We want to avoid what we fear because we assume those experiences will bring negative feelings.

Our judgments of others and ourselves – and it's almost impossible not to judge – are based on whether they meet the standards we hold in our minds, consciously or subconsciously.

Our fears and hopes about the future, and our focus on what we consider past negative experiences, keep us from fully enjoying and participating in the present. We chronically believe that the best is yet to come. But if the best always is in the future, does it ever really arrive, or has living for the future become a means of depriving ourselves of appreciating this moment? By our habitual thinking that the future is where our satisfaction lies, do we condemn ourselves to perpetual dissatisfaction? And does our putting off appreciating what we are given in the moment mean we will lead a life of discontent right up to the end?

The alternative is allowing ourselves the full experience of what happens in this moment, and then this one, and then the next. Once we did that but then learned to hold on to our ideas about the past and relive them. There always will be good times and bad. Our actual ongoing experience defies description, which makes it difficult to find the words – and lessons – for how to conduct ourselves in a way that will bring greater satisfaction.

Our words serve as anchors to help us know who and where we are; removing them can feel like the death of our functioning self. When we have what we consider significant insights we want to put them into words so we can retain what we have learned. But there is no way to adequately describe the present moment, and our best efforts tend to put our ongoing experience into categories that never are adequate or accurate.

How, then, do we function without the guidelines and guardrails we have adopted throughout life? We don't and can't. But when we keep in mind that those tools we have created to navigate our ship – our words and concepts – are not reality themselves, they no longer dominate our lives. Our original joy – based in feeling and not concepts – begins to return.

Our ideas about the past can be valuable as guides for the future, but turning them into a mandate for how we must live robs us of joy and creativity. We can see every ongoing moment as new if willing to open our eyes to embrace the reality before us, rather than simply considering the present a repeat of times past.

Our thoughts about our final destination also are a rehash of what we've seen or heard. Those ideas vary from reincarnation, to reunion with relatives, to ascent to the company of a god in the sky, to union with all of reality, to nothing at all. Despite claims made based on faith and limited experience, no one actually has died – except temporarily – and returned to tell their story. No one has come back with clear evidence of what lies on the other side.

What we can say with some confidence is that if we are unable to live joyously in this lifetime, suddenly learning to do so on another plane seems unlikely. Being able to bring enjoyment to our everyday experience is the most significant skill we can develop other than those we need to survive.

What keeps us from doing that is holding on to rigid ideas from the past about how we should live and imposing them on ourselves and others as we move into the future. Since the reality of who we are, who others are, and the nature of the world lie outside our concepts, paying respectful attention to all we encounter is what we most need to successfully confront what life brings. No matter how prepared we may believe ourselves, reality always will surprise us.

Death is easy: Of what use is life?
To die is to rest.

– Fijian poem[32]

Rites of Passage

In every culture we know of, rites of passage that mark the major stages of life are acknowledged by the community. These include birth, puberty, marriage, parenthood, entering into one's career, senior citizen status, and death.[33]

These rites remind us of our place in human society, where we all enact similar patterns from our beginning to our end. Their purpose is to acknowledge one's arrival at significant milestones. Rites can be formal, as is traditional in religious groups, or stages of maturity simply can be acknowledged by community members.

Rites are commemorations of the cyclical nature of life through which we all pass. The identity of each of us is largely defined by the stage into which we have entered and find ourselves until passage to the next.

Birth marks the time when the community acknowledges joint responsibility for raising a child who is expected to eventually contribute back. Bringing up children to honor traditional customs is the role not only of parents, but becomes a responsibility of the entire community, including its educational system. The child's creativity is encouraged, but in traditional societies there is an expectation that there will be no deviation from established norms. There is general agreement that traditions must be carried forward, not only because of custom, but for survival of the society itself.

Acknowledgement of puberty is customary in most societies and religions. Becoming a teenager is understood as the stage between childhood and adulthood. Childlike impulsiveness hopefully is left behind, but the self-control and responsibility for one's actions expected of adults is not yet fully in place. That is why adolescents in industrialized societies usually are not considered responsible for crimes they commit, except for the most serious offenses. In many religions and societies, the importance of adolescence is marked by specific rituals that acknowledge expectation of the end of childishness and an assumption of greater personal responsibility.[34]

At a set age in Western societies, usually 18

or 21, and at varying points in primitive cultures, one is expected to be capable of mature adult decisions and to enter on the path toward establishing a career or vocation. With lengthening lifespans in industrialized nations, the age at which one is expected to settle into a career gradually has risen. But in those societies where hunting and warrior skills still are considered a primary means of survival, and the lifespan is relatively short, the age of what is considered maturity remains around 16 to 18 years of age.

Marriage, considered essential for continuity of the race in most societies, has traditionally been common soon after one becomes an adult capable of raising a family.[35] But in industrialized nations, marriage is being put off until later years for many, and never entered into for a growing number of individuals, some of whom remain single or assume non-marriage relationships. This has resulted in a lower birth rate, which threatens the custom of having enough working people to contribute toward the sustenance of those in retirement. A married person is considered capable of fulfilling a long-term commitment, especially that which is required for raising and providing for children.

The divorce rate in industrialized societies has climbed over the years. But among some societies the choice of mate never was given to individuals. The Roman Catholic Church still forbids divorce, the Eastern Orthodox Church only allows divorce in extreme cases such as adultery, abuse, or abandonment, whereas in Judaism and the Muslim religion divorce is more easily obtained.

In most industrialized societies, retirement is considered an earned right. The official retirement age varies among countries, but is tending to be later as people live longer and the cost of retirement benefits increases. Different retirement systems are in place to provide sustenance to seniors, including Social Security in the United States, which people pay into as insurance during their working years. Basic health insurance is automatically provided for all in many countries, and for retirees in the US for those who don't have their own plan. Senior citizen status is considered an honored position in most countries with special discounts given for many types of purchases. In more traditional societies, the elderly are part of a family group, which means they are automatically cared for due to the closeness of younger family members. With aging, the impulsiveness of earlier years lessens, partly because of hormonal changes, and perhaps also due to life's lessons learned.[36]

As one advances in age, the inevitability of death looms. Planning for one's end is a major decision-making process that takes considerable thought, as does coming to grips with one's attitude about what lies on the other side, if anything. For those who know the end is coming, they must consider whether to make a conscious effort to adjust their attitude toward life and others, or take their relationship patterns with them to the grave. Over half the deaths in the US are caused by an illness that gives people time to look back and contemplate their life.[37] This provides an opportunity for them to change their relating patterns or examine their views of how they see themselves and others before arriving on their death bed.

What we consider the stages of life actually are constructs we use to enhance our understanding and communication. When we closely watch our progression, and that of others, we see that the entire life cycle is one of continuity. There also is an ongoing continuance of our essential selves that is the same now as five or fifty years ago, and will be the same five or fifty years hence, despite changes in our appearance and views. Rites of passage are reminders of stages of status in society, but ignore the reality that we always have been and always will be the same essential individual.

Some Eastern religions and individuals of many faiths hold the view that we enter this life after a series of previous incarnations, and that each incarnation is an attempt at self-perfection. Some religions, like Roman Catholicism, teach that living an exemplary life on earth prepares us for the hereafter, while others, like fundamentalist Christianity, teach that seeking God's forgiveness for our actions on earth eases the soul for passage to the afterlife.

While many religions see rites of passage as a framework for the development of the soul, many people in Western societies are leaving religion altogether. They tend to believe that what governs human beings is our biology, and that the essence of a person, if any, dies with the body. How do we sort all this out?

When we look at the evidence for the origin of life on earth – of which we only are a small part – we see that in the long view, it began a billion or more years ago, then slowly evolved into multicellular forms, and only recently, in geologic terms, developed the complex beings we see today. What remains hidden from our perspective of a single lifetime is that the process of slow change continues both around and within us. The elements of which we are composed have been arranged in the bodies of creatures that have come before us, and now are arranged within us in a similar manner. Those elements – oxygen carbon, hydrogen, nitrogen, calcium, and phosphorus – continually shift into and out of our bodies in exchange with our surroundings.[38]

Thus we are not just part of the universe, but the universe itself. So the question of our origins and destination become clear from understanding that we always have been and will be the ever-changing reality that is all around and within us. Our ability to describe our real nature becomes lost in the words we use in the contemplation of that reality. It would be accurate to say that there only is one incarnation and we are it.

We each have taken on the role of individuals with a body, mind and essential self that some call the soul. That understanding is not a cause for depression or despair. It leads to the realization that the bodies we think of as our selves are an appearance from which we choose to interact with the world. It also clarifies that we share this universe as equals with every other human being, and confirms our understanding that we have a common essential nature. In the longer view, awareness of our real nature grants us eternal life. We then can use that knowledge to guide us in our everyday functioning and interactions.

HOW TO DIE

Knowledge is acquired when we succeed in fitting a new experience into the system of concepts based upon our old experiences. Understanding comes when we liberate ourselves from the old and so make possible a direct, unmediated contact with the new, the mystery, moment by moment, of our existence.

– Aldous Huxley[39]

Exceeding Ourselves

We once experienced a deep connection with all that is around us when we didn't know of a separation between us and the world.[40] Then we learned to label everything and everyone, including ourselves. We began believing that we and others are those labels, while ignoring what we actually see. In our minds we became separate beings living in a world of separate things.

In our earliest years our creativity and spontaneity are boundless. But once we construct a self-image, we begin to restrict ourselves and our actions to the concept we have come to believe in. Our original creative selves become largely suppressed. We avoid going beyond safe boundaries for fear of losing the person we have created ourselves to be. We think in terms of what we can and cannot do based on how we observe ourselves act and how others describe us.

Then, throughout our lives, we seek recognition for our lost original selves. We may never experience that recognition because we have learned to keep our hidden part locked away for fear of being different from the carefully constructed self we present to the world.

But that place within us we deny doesn't go away. It continually vies for attention. It includes the infinite creativity we expressed when young; seeing the world for ourselves rather than through the eyes of others; our ability to connect with people by recognizing their joyful essence; the spontaneity we learned to control to live up to our society's idea of who we should be.

Some creative individuals remain in touch with the inner source that many of us suppress. They often are misunderstood or condemned by society, or even by a part of themselves. Writers and artists who live in both worlds often are torn between the two. They still see their original world while struggling to live in the one they were taught is real. The result is conflict at best, and a divided person driven to self-harm at worst. We only need to think of famous people who have self-destructed as a result of their inner conflicts.

But we continue to carry within us an intuition of the way we once saw the world, and hope to have that original self recognized. And we all, at times, blame others for failing to provide us the recognition we seek.

The rebelliousness of original thinkers often becomes expressed in behavior that says: "Why don't you see the world as I do?" But once enough people recognize their insight, it can result in a new shared vision of reality. We begin to realize there is a different – and often better – way to see. Science, architecture, art, music, and other fields are changed and progress due to those who see the world differently. A few daring thinkers come to mind: in science, Galileo, Newton, and Einstein; in architecture, Frank Loyd Wright and the Bauhaus artists;[41] in art, Van Gogh and Picasso; in music, Mozart and Philip Glass; in literature, James Joyce and Virginia Woolf. In his classic treatment of scientific discoveries, Thomas Kuhn called a change in a society's accepted views a "paradigm shift."[42]

Along with our creative side, we carry a judgmental self within that evolution designed to make us responsible members of our tribe or society. It includes the rules and mores we are taught and enables us to function in collaboration with others. Without it we could not accomplish our common goals. It is the basis of our educational system and economy.

For many of us, we limit our views to the most common perspective and fail to see beyond that which is already established. We cut off our potential for the expression of our creative self.

An alternative is looking beyond our limited perspective. Doing this can seem risky; we may fear entering what seems like unknown territory. When we recognize the creative potential within us, a long-dormant part begins to awaken that we remember with excitement. But we also fear that the carefully constructed self we have learned to present to the world may die.

Without shocking ourselves too greatly we can begin to move beyond the mental straitjacket into which we have voluntarily climbed. We can begin to actually look at the world and see that what surrounds us – and lies within – does not fall into our set categories. Flowers, trees, and people – including ourselves – are much more than the labels we place on them. Our life is vastly improved by our recognition and interaction with their essence rather than with our concepts of them.

To move toward greater fulfillment we could start by making small efforts. We can pay more attention and see more of what actually is there when we keep in mind that our concepts are not reality itself. Then we can begin to move beyond our self-imposed limits.

In the interpersonal realm, we might consider our interactions. Do we see people in terms of preset ideas, or can we have more rewarding experiences if we open our minds to the person beyond our concepts? With those we know, as well as those we don't, can we hear beyond the words and listen for the emotional expression behind them? Can we recognize the essence of people beyond what they actually are saying?

We never can assume that our impression of anyone is the reality of who they are. We can practice opening our minds and hearts as if we don't know them, and, except in our concepts, we really don't. But occasionally we may find we need to avoid someone because of chronic harmful behavior.

A flexible mental view toward others and the world correlates with a healthy brain and body according to much modern research.[43] When engaged in chronic cynicism, we negatively affect our brain and body, which can lead to multiple physical issues. When open to others and willing to adjust our views, it correlates with improved blood flow and a healthier heart.[44]

Our emotions can move us closer or farther from our families and everyone else, which greatly affects our health and quality of life. We can slowly learn to remove the barriers we have created to our connections if we practice this on an everyday basis.

In the physical realm, we best can take care of ourselves by a regular routine that pushes us a bit beyond our normal zone of comfort. Exercise of any type that races the heart and adds strength without hurting us is likely to lead to a longer life. Stretching to interrupt long periods of sitting also is crucial.

Spirituality is our unseen relationship with what is outside of us. It can be experienced in love between us and others, interplay with the forces of nature, or contemplation of the universe. Spirituality is awareness of our connection with everyone and everything, or with what some call God, which can have different meanings for different people. Spiritual awareness takes our emphasis away from our problems and moves our focus to the larger continuity of time and nature, which is just as valid a view.

Moving beyond our self-imposed limits can

greatly improve our lives. There is nothing we do that is only "mental." Every activity also happens somewhere in our bodies. Expanding our horizons – especially increased socialization and acceptance of others – has the potential to positively affect our brains and extend our lifespans.[45]

It's never too late to expand our ideas and interactions beyond our current habits and perceptions. This also applies to how we see ourselves; rigidity on the outside corresponds with rigidity on the inside. But moving beyond where we always have been in our views and actions brings us closer to our original flexibility, which correlates with better health.

As we open ourselves to more of the truth of others and our surroundings, rather than remaining stuck in our old views, we begin fulfilling the most essential part of ourselves: that which longs to be recognized. So in every area of your life, challenge yourself to move beyond your comfort limits. It will make you feel – and actually become – more alive and will set a pattern for improving the rest of your life.

HOW TO DIE

Last scene of all,
That ends this strange eventful history,
Is second childishness and mere oblivion;
Sans teeth, sans eyes, sans taste, sans everything.

– FINAL LINES OF "ALL THE WORLD'S A STAGE,"
FROM AS YOU LIKE IT, BY WILLIAM SHAKESPEARE

Living And Dying Well

I've heard it said we only die once. The evidence seems to lend truth to that rumor. So perhaps we might consider how best we can live with our life's end in mind.

Of this we can be certain: we will make mistakes, miscalculate, and mess up due to the limits of our perceptions and emotional attachment to views that often make us inflexible. So our only real choice is whether to blame or forgive ourselves. We can apologize to those we have offended and try to learn from our mistakes, but we are likely to repeat them before long.

Failure to forgive ourselves can be a chronic destructive pattern that we carry with us. Hardly a day goes by when I don't make a miscalculation based on my limited understanding of the present or mistaken predictions of what the future will bring.

A pattern of blame also can apply to our interactions. No one I know – or don't know – likely lives up to my standards. Events often fail to go in my desired direction. The government I live under falls short of how I think it should operate and treat me. So my choice is whether to focus on the shortcomings of those around me, those who influence me, and my fate, or to realize that shortcomings are an inescapable part of what I am likely to experience during my sojourn on this earth.

Our personal hell is the same hell described by many religions. They consider human suffering to be caused by a source outside of ourselves. Many people hope to escape that fate by union with a higher being – in the present or after death. But we rarely are aware that our own hell usually is self-imposed by comparing the conditions of our lives with an unattainable ideal. As mentioned, the only time we can do anything is in the present. So we might ask what we are doing right now to bring ourselves forgiveness.

Rather than being imposed on us, we are bringing ourselves our feelings at this moment.

If we recall a time of unhappiness, or anticipate a bad experience, it happens for us now. If we are dwelling on a good memory or contemplating a time we hope to be at peace, that is our current experience. This is what we always have done, and in the future we likely will do the same.

We alter our own moods by what we remember or anticipate. Our minds wander alternately to the contemplation of what we hope and fear. When young we moved between moods by simply allowing them to be there, but began to believe we are stable persons with consistent moods. The reality is that there is an ever-changing parade of thoughts cascading through our minds. When we allow – or forgive – our thoughts and feelings they move on and lose their grip.

Our current state of mind – positive or negative – only is temporary. We can alter it by allowing it to be there, as contradictory as that may sound. This is another way of saying that, even when we are at our very worst, we can choose to forgive ourselves and move on. Otherwise we condemn ourselves to a perpetual pattern of self-blame.

But real forgiveness is more than a word or concept. It is a feeling that reverberates through us and cleanses us of negativity. It allows us to start over. Many religious rituals are based on this idea.[46] But before long we once again commit another act for which we need to forgive ourselves, so this is a habit we must cultivate.

Forgiveness has a physical effect on our health. When not forgiving I am tense; my muscles tighten and the flow of blood throughout my body and brain becomes constricted.[47] This is why chronic stress has the potential to threaten our health. When I am forgiving, my body becomes relaxed; my blood flows well and my heart opens up.[48]

But doing this is more easily said than done.

Blame is a habit we have learned and practiced throughout our lives. Forgiveness is a way of being about which we must continually remind ourselves. We first must become clear about what forgiveness is, and why it's essential for our mental and physical health, regardless of the situation.

In the world of blame we judge people by standards they never can meet, even if they knew what our standards are. But as we do this we also experience isolation and judgment.

In the world of forgiveness we respect others and do our best to make improvements based on agreements, knowing we likely will fall off the path again. That will require ongoing communication and a willingness to forgive once again.

To maintain our peace of mind, we need to be aware that we can't ever live up to the expectations we hold for ourselves. We set standards, fall short, get up, and try again. Others can be harsh on us as well as on themselves. So we remind ourselves that self-forgiveness only can come from within.

What about those high achievers who have attained enviable status in our eyes? Certainly they have peace of mind?

Human nature is such that no one ever achieves enough to satisfy our inner critic. Our ideal of how we and the world should be always is beyond us. A glimpse at many great achievers who lead stressful lives should make this clear. Our heroes – in fields from politics, to athletics, to literature, to art, to music – often collapse in a heap of self-destruction.

Perhaps we can let those who speak to us from their deathbeds remind us of how our better selves really want to be. People in that situation often express regret at not having been more forgiving, loving or generous.[49]

For them, it's too late to relive their lives. But for us – with practice and some determination – we can live lives of forgiveness. That is our most basic view to which we long to return. And the only time we can do that is in the present moment.

When we bring ourselves a feeling of forgiveness in the present, it also applies to times in the future when we are certain to fall short. So in a way, real forgiveness is for all time.

That doesn't mean we don't learn from our mistakes and try to improve how we approach the world and interact with others. Sometimes the lessons need to be ground in, as when we put ourselves in precarious situations or act in a way that causes us to become isolated from others. Some people even need to be incarcerated to protect others from their impulsiveness. But the feeling of forgiveness makes us less bitter and reactive and also less likely to repeat our mistakes. We may try to learn and improve, but for many situations we get just one chance. So our only real saving grace is forgiving ourselves, which allows us to move on with our lives. Or we can wait for forgiveness from others that may never be forthcoming.

Our real selves are not the limited beings we believe them to be. The real self sees who we have become but is the same entity as when we started.

When we look forward to our final moments, we anticipate separation from the earth of the person we believe ourselves to be. We imagine a state of being where we no longer function as we have during our lifetime. It seems likely that our final act will be letting go of all we know and experience.

But we can learn now from what that state of letting go might teach us. Releasing our attachments to guilt, blame, and all other negative emotions sets us free. It allows us to make choices about the direction of our lives based more on reality than the patterns we have learned that often defeat us. But perhaps most importantly, it puts us back in touch with the original view that we have forgotten.

Once we let go of our attachments to this life we find it easy to discuss – and even joke about – death because it no longer holds a grip on us. This allows us to participate more emotionally and fully in the reality of each moment free of our ultimate fear.[50]

The self that is attached to our idea of how the world should be begins to fade when we encounter reality as we find it. And the joy of this experience allows us to move on to the next encounter, and then the next.

HOW TO DIE

*None are more hopelessly enslaved than those
who falsely believe they are free.*

– JOHANN WOLFGANG VON GOETHE

The Nature Of Freedom

No person or situation can grant us freedom. In the worst of times we hope for things to improve. In the best of times we tend to focus on what is wrong rather than appreciating our situation. You might ask yourself when you last said or thought: "These really are good times."

There always have been autocratic states that dominated people's lives. Throughout history we have struggled to overcome oppression. But revolutions rarely have resulted in improving the lives of those who consider themselves oppressed. Often there has been a reduction in freedom under the new regime. Two examples: the 1917 Russian Revolution resulted in the Soviet Union under whose oppression millions died; the 1949 revolution in China led to a greater and more onerous suppression of human rights, also resulting in the deaths of millions.

Oppressive regimes often come into place by democratic means. People commonly vote for change amidst real or perceived economic downturns. After the First World War, Germany was an advanced culture steeped in great art, science and philosophy, but economically depressed. Support was strong for a political movement that promised to make the country great again, but people failed to consider ominous signs of the eventual loss of their freedom in the speeches of their leader.[51]

After the collapse of the Soviet Union in 1991, Russians looked forward to participating in a free society. But economic chaos resulted in support for a strong autocracy rather than democracy.[52]

In the United States during the 2024 election, many people felt victimized by high inflation and voted the party out of power they held responsible for their difficulty in making ends meet. But they failed to be swayed by the fact that the eventual victor had promised to suspend the Constitution and stated: "You won't have to vote anymore."[53]

Voters often consider their economic situation above all else. They ignore warning signs by their expected rescuers of a move toward autocracy. They think their own oppression is unlikely even when politicians stigmatize others. And, perhaps most importantly, they have no clear concept of the democratic vision they hope will improve their lives.

What most people fail to understand is that the government they live under, no matter whether it meets their ideal, never can provide fulfillment. They equate economic prosperity with personal satisfaction. They fail to remember that – even in the best of times – their government cannot guarantee them the peace of mind they seek because that never has been the realm of government, or any other of our circumstances.

We all want to live in situations that maximize our opportunities and prosperity. We want a government that grants us the greatest possible amount of freedom to conduct the lives we choose. And we want to overthrow autocratic governments that fail to honor the dignity of those they govern.

Because people believe that their circumstances determine their happiness, they think they are one and the same. We rarely are taught there is a difference between the two, but if we really pay attention we find that even when things go well for us we rarely, if ever, are able to secure long-term peace of mind, only to be disillusioned by one situation after another that fails to provide what we most want.

A real sense of freedom is not brought to us by the situation in which we live. It is not a result of getting things we want. Those who have oppression lifted often have a brief experience of freedom. But before long the mind focuses again on what is missing.

No matter our circumstances and how free or oppressive the environment in which we live, we choose to bring ourselves a feeling of appreciation for life or dwell on its shortcomings. In our society the emphasis on what is lacking is far more prevalent than on appreciating the life we live.

In his book, *Man's Search for Meaning*, Victor Frankl tells us:

Everything can be taken from a man but one thing: the last of the human freedoms—to choose one's attitude in any given set of circumstances, to choose one's own way.[54]

Frankl, who spent three years in concentration camps during World War II, wrote that he had faith in the common decency within every human being. That quality may remain hidden, but often it emerges in small ways. Despite learning to act evil, no one is evil at core.

This is similar to the view expressed by Nelson Mandela in *Long Walk to Freedom*:

To be free is not merely to cast off one's chains,

but to live in a way that respects and enhances the freedom of others.[55]

While imprisoned for 27 years for revolutionary activities, Mandela began to see everyone, including his prison guards, as "a glimmer of humanity...Man's goodness is a flame that can be hidden but never extinguished."[56]

Real freedom exists in the minds and souls of individuals; it is not granted to us by the circumstances of our lives. No method, no technique, and no teaching can bring us freedom; only an understanding of how we enslave ourselves with our own thoughts.

Freedom is not only an idea, but the feeling of knowing our worth. Those most confident in that quality also see it in others, regardless of how others see themselves and the world.

We seek a life for which we can be grateful. But allowing ourselves gratitude for the life we have – or even parts of it – changes it from a state of anticipation to one of fulfillment.[57]

Once secure in our inner freedom – the only real freedom there is – we can bring that into our interactions with others and the world. We can extend our valuing of ourselves into valuing all that is around us. We can use it as a guide to forging a political structure that is most likely to value every human being. Some call this democracy.

When truly free we recognize our own value and that of others. We contribute to the kind and compassionate world in which we want to live rather than to one of blame and recrimination. Even when we fail at this we acknowledge our imperfections and allow ourselves to move on.

When we or our cultures do not understand the importance of valuing people it leads to conflict. Many wars have been fought within and between nations to defend individual rights and dignity. The United Nations was formed to build on the lessons from two world wars.

There has been much debate about the nature of intelligence. Is it an ability to do well at tests, to compete with others, to solve problems, to get along with people, to navigate one's environment? It seems to me that the real value of human intelligence is to move us toward a better world – one that has the potential to elevate every human being. When people use their intelligence to serve humanity, rather than compete with others or enhance their war skills, our civilization has moved forward.

When we have used our freedom to acknowledge the value of others we have advanced. Progress in human rights and technology go together. Within the last 200 years there have been more advances in technology and human rights – mainly in democracies – that did not happen in the previous 5000 years.

We are not nearly at the end of our struggle to make the world a place that honors the integrity of every human being. Perhaps we are only at the beginning. The world of our dreams is off imperceptibly in the future. The forces of resistance are formidable both within and without us. We only can build confidently toward that future when fortified by the knowledge that the inner satisfaction sought by every human being is the same as our own, and that they are interconnected. This view then can be expressed in both how we interact personally and the realm of our politics.

There will be setbacks. We will be told that the world we seek is a dream and we will be tempted to give up. But over time we have moved closer to a universal recognition of human dignity and will continue to do so as more of us become committed to that vision. And as we do so our own value as human beings – and of all human beings – will continue to gain recognition.

The time to start is now.

HOW TO DIE

Who has lived in dignity, dies in dignity.
– SHERWIN B NULAND[58]

The Best Years of our Lives

Some people think the best years of their lives lie behind them in a carefree youth, while others believe their best years are in the future through rewarding relationships, satisfying work, or a restful retirement. But for most of us, as we grow older, the fulfillment we hoped for seems to elude us.

Throughout my youth, I looked forward to a time when I would at last be competent, wise, smart, or strong enough to experience fulfillment. Then at some point, rather than looking forward, I began to glimpse back at what seemed like my best years. Eventually I realized I was telling myself I am not capable of full enjoyment and participation in life in the moment. It always seemed to be at some other time.

I began to see that the tenets of our culture – as expressed by our language – perpetuated that view. Our descriptions of what we most want refer to the past or future, rather than bringing us an experience of fulfillment in the present.

We talk about attaining success at some point. We say we want a more loving world but don't discuss how to bring that about. We refer to a time when we believe things were better. But if we always think fulfillment is at another time, we omit the possibility of experiencing it in this moment.

Most of our discussions – one on one or in group settings – focus on the shortcomings around us, how much better things were in the past, or hopefully will be some day. Reference to an idealized past or future is seen in every political platform, spiritual view, historical perspective, philosophy, and psychological prescription.

We often discuss problems but rarely devote energy to solutions and how they might be accomplished. Even more rarely do we consider what it would do for us personally if the world were to meet our hopes or expectations.

At some point I realized that my focus on an idealized past or future did little to improve my life in the present. I began to pay more attention to what was happening around me, although my habit of focusing elsewhere usually still dominated my consciousness. It became clear that seeking fulfillment is what kept me from experiencing it. By watching myself over time I was able to see that personal satisfaction was the result of the attitude I brought with me to my experience and not a result of the experience itself.

For most of us, our lives are overloaded with problems and issues. In my life – and most likely in yours – there are a myriad of daily challenges that must be confronted.

In our day, self-improvement has become a perpetual pursuit for many. It also has become a big business. For those seeking greater satisfaction, it is fashionable to try to bring ourselves into the present via practices such as yoga, exercise, meditation and the admonition to "be here now." Many people get involved in various types of spiritual practice.

Those under oppressive governments crave living in a democracy with the assumption it will bring them fulfillment. Those of us who live in democracies face a continual threat of whether we will be able to maintain them. But democracy itself never has – and never will – guarantee us the satisfaction we seek. As long as we habitually focus on what is lacking, that is what we will experience. We look to the future and past as fulfillment eludes us in the present. We hope for the world to be different as we blame others and circumstances for our dissatisfaction.

Our long history of wars is the result of people trying to gain control over others they consider a threat. But removing threats never can bring us the peace we seek. Rather, it is brought to us by learning to cultivate it in our minds and souls. Then, as we become more secure in that feeling, we can bring it into our lives and relationships.

So what is that feeling? It is a mental state where we no longer look to others to confirm our value as human beings; where we don't wait for circumstances to change, but allow the emotional experience we most want into our lives. It is no longer waiting for the world to bring us fulfillment.

The circumstances of our lives may or may not change in the direction we want them to go. But there are two parts to every experience. One is what happens; we can control some of that and some we cannot. Circumstances have a way of surprising us regardless of our best-laid plans.

The second part of every experience is at the level of feeling. Our encounters with others and the world seem to buffet us between good feelings and bad. But even if we stay in one place and avoid encountering the world, our minds vary between positive and negative emotions all on their own.

There is another part of us that seeks

recognition. It is that which witnesses both our outer and inner experience. It is what some call our essence or soul. It always is and has been the same; our most essential identity that we often ignore as we try to change our world and selves to bring us greater satisfaction. As we learn to recognize that essential self regardless of what we encounter, we begin to see it is not circumstances that determine our happiness, but our decision to acknowledge that part of ourselves.

As children most of us usually received positive recognition no matter what we did. Then we learned there are actions that bring the attention we seek, and other actions that cause it to be denied. We even would usually prefer negative recognition to none.

Our history of emotions has become part of our identity. We remember incidents not so much for themselves as for how they affected us, and still do, when we recall them.[59] We continually bring memories of both positive and negative experiences to mind. We then try to recreate the positive in our perpetual quest for fulfillment.

But there is another route to fulfillment. It is recognizing our essential self regardless of what happens and bringing that into our experience as we realize that our actions – and the world – never will do that for us. It is allowing ourselves a feeling of validity rather than waiting for it to be provided. It is a willingness to allow ourselves inner peace – if only for this moment – as we stop seeking it from the outside. But that involves the death of our identity as a perpetual seeker.

Peace of mind is our most natural state, but habitually seeking it pulls us off center. Seeking it really is saying we currently do not experience it; perpetual seeking puts it off indefinitely into the future. Dwelling on negative memories – and even on positive hopes – do not lead us to the experience of fulfillment.

If we choose, we can recognize that the best years – and moments – of our lives are not behind or ahead of us. We harm ourselves by denying us the experience of peace in this moment. When we stop working to bring ourselves fulfillment we find we are more relaxed, we breathe more easily, and are more at peace with ourselves, others and the world. We no longer seek what we most want because we realize it already is our most natural state. Then, if we desire, we can bring that understanding into the next activity or path upon which we embark.

Any Day Now, Any Day Now,
I Shall Be Released

– Bob Dylan[60]

The Final Transition

As we progress through the stages of our lives, we only begin to notice the changes that have taken place when we look back. Throughout our journey there is a continuous essential self that witnesses it all. The transitions from youth to adulthood to senior status to old age exist more in our recollections than the reality of everyday living.

We remember key moments that define our idea of who we are. Our memory is a torrent of experiences we recall in random order, depending on where our recollections take us. We retain the emotional content of episodes that hit us most strongly.[61] Positive encounters, bitter disappointments, experiences of love, domination by anger, serene moments, and haunting regrets alternate with awareness of our current surroundings and daily tasks.

Our feelings seem automatic: they sometimes come from reactions to events and sometimes from within. By embracing what courses through our minds we are able to move on to what comes next. Otherwise our memories can dominate us, sometimes against our will.

As we approach what we think of as our final stage we experience a narrowing of our capacity to function. The emotional component that gives life meaning seems to fade. But regardless of our need to slow down physically and mentally, we still can bring a fullness of feeling to our encounters. There is a difference between believing who we are and knowing who we are. When we watch ourselves without judgment we find that at our core we are the same person we always have been.

A great deal of research has been done about how to maintain viability in our later years. Results show that the attitudes and habits that make life most enjoyable are the same at all stages. The advice of researchers include maintaining daily physical exercise to the extent possible, emphasizing good nutrition, and participating in activities that result in mental stimulation.[62]

But recent studies show that the most reliable predictor of longevity is relationships. A predominant recommendation is to maintain a network of positive social contacts.[63] What do our interactions with others have to do with physical health and longevity? The answer lies in how the mind and body work.

Most of us believe that our minds are different from our bodies – that the mind exists in some uncertain place, perhaps in the brain; it contemplates us, others and the universe. It seems that the mind is not subject to physical wear and tear as is the body.

But in reality, our thoughts are experienced in our bodies. Our stress can be measured by the tools of modern medical science, including blood pressure, heart rate, and EEG (electroencephalography). In our everyday functioning we detect the stress levels of others by how tense they look, and of ourselves by how tense we feel. Our stress increases or decreases based on whether or not events correspond to how we would like them to go. Our family lives, jobs, and everyday encounters can add to – or subtract from – the amount of stress we feel.[64]

So how we think about events – both positively and negatively – affects us and the quality of our experience. Our peace of mind or stress depends on the connection or lack of connection we experience in our interactions.

Research shows that those who feel connected

to others are likely to experience greater peace of mind, as well as better physical health.[65] Those who feel isolated are more likely to have chronic tension, which leads to constriction of the flow of blood and nutrients while accelerating the aging process.

Although studies point in the direction of greater social contact, they rarely recommend how to increase it in our lives. What they overlook is the individual choices we make.

We all feel connected to others at times and isolated at times. So how do we develop a lifestyle that maximizes positive interactions? Are some people fortunate enough to have more social contacts, or is connection with others a skill we can develop? To explore those questions let's go back to the beginning of our lives – and the beginning of this book.

We usually think that our life's quality is the result of whether we have a nurturant upbringing, whether the daily factors that affect us are favorable, whether we live in a country that guarantees our freedom to develop our talents and skills. We also think that satisfaction is a result of whether we make maximum use of the abilities we find within. We know there are people born in poverty who seem successful and happy, and that some born in an atmosphere of privilege stumble uncertainly through life.

Regardless of how we appear to others, we all have times of success and disappointment, happiness and sadness, emotional highs and lows. We also have been convinced by our society to not acknowledge those times when our minds, perhaps for reasons unknown, seem to pull us down to an unwelcome place. We – and those around us – believe that success, however we understand it, will lead to happiness, and failure will bring unhappiness. But our actual experience does not always correlate with those expectations.

Our moods vary, sometimes in response to events and at other times seemingly on their own. But here's where social interaction comes in: if we are involved in positive interpersonal relationships we are more likely to accept the ups and downs of our minds and those of others.

As children, most of us assumed support from our parents and freely expressed our discontent, sometimes based on need and sometimes seeming to come out of us for no reason. But regardless of becoming adults, our moodiness really has not left us. Our minds never have quite come under control – despite appearances – as we have become expert at hiding what we think and feel.

As our emotions course through us – often unwelcome – there is a cost to hiding them. It requires tension to keep from expressing the feelings we suppress, and then when we express them angrily, more tension accompanies our anger.[66]

In the company of supportive social networks we are likely to have less anger and to accept and express our emotions in a positive manner. This benefits our health as we experience a connection with others rather than suffer in isolation. That is why studies show that those who live in supportive situations are likely to be happier, healthier and live longer.

In many traditional societies large numbers of family members continue to interact and support each other throughout their lifespans. In Western societies, however, people often live alone or in smaller family groups. Many need assistance in the activities of daily living and require medical care. They find themselves in nursing homes or other situations where they are dependent on others. Their social interactions with people are limited or absent.

To address that issue a number of alternative models are being tried. Living situations that combine individuals of different age groups provide interactions unlike traditional nursing homes, usually with good results. Some of these "intergenerational housing models" include intentional communities and housing for older adults on college campuses.[67] The hope is that younger community members can benefit from the experience of interactions with their elders, and that older adults can enjoy the spontaneity of those who are younger.

Another alternative to traditional senior housing is being explored by the MIT AgeLab, as described in the book *Longevity Hubs*. The idea is that communities can be designed to include seniors in their social and economic life. According to the authors: "What's needed now are communities willing to cultivate a critical mass of age-integrating innovations so people all across the life course can find proximity and shared purpose in the course of daily life....In some of the most vibrant older populations around the world, healthy living tends to coincide with continuous learning, as well as regular interactions among older and younger generations."[68]

Our degree of interaction with others is a choice. Our psychology, religions, and philosophy have a common goal of removing barriers to healthful interaction. Regardless of our background, we each choose to remain in isolation in our minds or to appreciate our connections to others.[69]

Early in life we determine which group or groups to which we belong and those with whom we are willing to relate. We often limit our connections to those groups. Thus we choose to identify with some people, while cutting ourselves off from those outside the groups with which we believe we can comfortably interact.

But when we expand beyond our usual comfort zone to greater connectedness with others, we return to the view with which we were born. As we do that in our minds, we no longer depend on what happens to us to determine our peace of mind. We create that first, and then bring it into our interactions.

This is not as difficult as it may seem. At this moment, for whoever you are contemplating in your mind, you see yourself connected or disconnected. Connection is not only a feeling, but a physical sensation by which we open ourselves to the world – we breathe more easily, we are more relaxed and have an experience of interaction. This is the mode by which we came into this life.

Connection is our most natural state. It's not something we need to manufacture, but we often block our awareness of it in our minds. As we do, our health and longevity become threatened.

Of course there are real dangers in the world – both human and natural – from which we must retreat if we are to avoid being harmed or to ensure we survive. There also are times when we may need to fight to defend ourselves or preserve our freedom. But we harm ourselves when we harbor chronic anger, hatred or suspicion.

There are many creation myths that tell us we once lived in a perfect world we were forced to abandon because of our behavior. History tells of peaceful times alternating with wars that hopefully serve as lessons for how we should now live. Our philosophies explore views we may use to improve our lives. Our psychology turns us inward in an attempt to understand and alleviate our chronic suffering. And our religions tell us how to return to that world.

Lessons in these areas are intended to steer us in a more peaceful direction – both as individuals and as a society. They are based on improving our interactions so we may live more happily and successfully.

But what has been missing in all this well-intentioned advice is what is most important: the feeling we seek behind our actions. We are admonished to treat others as we want to be treated. It would be hard to argue that is not good advice. But our actions – even based on the greatest teachings of the ages – don't necessarily yield the feeling we seek. Thus we move from one set of principles to another hoping the next will at last yield the emotional reward we are after.

Perhaps there is another view we might consider. Perhaps our continual focus on improving ourselves and our lives keeps us from experiencing the feeling we want in the present. And perhaps what we most want already is surging through us.

Although largely unaware of it, there is a person we have created over the course of our lives, with talents and skills and limitations. That person often keeps us from experiencing and expressing the essential self with which we were born.

The person we present to the world is a mask that conceals who we really are: the kind and loving essence that many – upon dying – rediscover and long to reveal to the world. But often that happens too late.

If we choose, we can recontact and evoke our essential self. But that would require the death of the separate individual obsessed with survival and status we have created ourselves to be and have lived out for most of our time on this planet.

The self beneath the façade is guided by a sense of connection. That self dwells in a state of interrelationship with the world and lives beyond the fear of physical death.

Throughout our lives our real self seeks to be reborn – a self of renewal, of seeing the world with fresh eyes, of spontaneity, of the youthfulness we once expressed, of the joy of discovery. It is the self that yearns to be awakened by the love potential inside us. As we shed the old self for the new, we evoke the world of our longing.

HOW TO DIE

Books Used for Reference

Being Mortal, Medicine and What Matters in the End, Atul Gawande, 2014, Holt.

The Body Keeps the Score: Brain, Mind, and Body in the Healing of Trauma, Bessel Van De Kolk, 2015, Penguin.

The Call to Adventure, Bringing the Hero's Journey to Everyday Life, Paul Rebillot, 1993, Harper Collins.

The Denial of Death, Ernest Becker, 1973, Free Press.

The Departure of the Soul According to the Teaching of the Orthodox Church, St. Anthony's Greek Orthodox Monastery, 2020, Sagam Press.

The Egyptian Book of the Dead, 2022, Sirius Publishing.

Elderhood: Redefining Aging, Transforming Medicine, Reimagining Life, Louise Aronson, 2019, Bloomsbury Publishing.

Fluke, Chance, Chaos, and Why Everything We Do Matters, Brian Klaas, 2024, Scribner.

The Future of Democracy, Steve Zolno, 2016, Regent Press.

How We Die; Reflections on Life's Final Chapter, Sherwin B Nuland, 1995, Vintage.

Leviathan, Thomas Hobbes, [1651], 1998, Oxford.

Life After Life, Raymond A. Moody, 1975, 2015, Harper.

Long Walk to Freedom: The Autobiography of Nelson Mandela, Nelson Mandela, 1994, Little, Brown.

Lost Connections, Understanding the Real Causes of Depression – and the Unexpected Solutions, Johann Hari, 2018, Bloomsbury.

Man's Search for Meaning, Viktor Frankl, 1959, 2006, Beacon Press.

The Nature of Prejudice, Gordon Allport, 1979, Perseus Books.

Politics, Aristotle, 1959, Everyman's Library.

Primitive Religion, Its Nature and Origin, Paul Radin, 1975, Dover.

The Rites of Passage, Arnold van Gennep, 1909, originally in French, 1960 English Translation, University of Chicago Press.

Books Used for Reference

Rosencranz and Guildenstern are Dead, Tom Stoppard, 1967, 2017, Grove Press.

The Story of Earth, Robert M. Hazen, 2013, Viking Penguin.

The Structure of Scientific Revolutions, Thomas Kuhn, 1962, 2012, University of Chicago Press.

Successful Aging, Daniel J. Levitin, 2020, Dutton.

The Tibetan Book of the Dead, Introductory Commentary by The Dalai Lama, 2007, Penguin.

Why We Cooperate, Michael Tomasello, 2009, Boston Review of Books.

Why We Remember, Charan Ranganath, 2024, Doubleday.

A Year To Live, How To Live This Year As If It Were Your Last, Stephen Levine, 1997, Three Rivers Press.

HOW TO DIE

Endnotes

1 *The Denial of Death*, Page 86: "The 'healthy' person...is the one who has transcended himself...by realizing the truth of his situation, by dispelling the lie of his character, by breaking his spirit out of its conditioned prison."

2 *The Denial of Death*, Pages 13-14: "Animals in order to survive have had to be protected by fear-responses, in relationship not only to other animals but to nature itself....Reality and fear go together naturally. Man's fears are fashioned out of the ways he sees the world."

3 In *Life After Life*, the author interviews 50 people who claimed to have "near death experiences," and then came back to describe what the author calls "life on the other side."

4 *Slate*, September 2, 2019, *How the controversy around a Christian bestseller engulfed the evangelical publishing industry — and tore a family apart:* " 'I Did Not Die. I Did Not Go to Heaven,' Alex Moody denied the premise of the book, *The Boy Who Came Back From Heaven*, that described his ascent to heaven in the company of angels after two months in a coma brought on by a nearly fatal traffic accident at age 6. He claimed in the article that his father had "concocted" the story.

5 Ashley Strickland, CNN, June 7, 2023: "Mysterious species buried their dead and carved symbols 100,000 years before humans."

6   *The Story of Earth*, Page 102

7   *The Story of Earth*, Page 5: "It took a half-million years for even the first atoms...to emerge from the cauldron of creation. Millions more years passed while gravity coaxed these primordial gases into the first nebulas, then collapsed the nebulas into the first hot, dense, incandescent stars...Everything that gives us shelter and sustenance, all the objects we possess, indeed every atom and molecule of our flesh-bound shells, comes from earth and will return to earth."

8   *The Story of Earth*, Page 79: "At the chaotic surface, roaring rivers and crashing waves became principal agents for the erosion of rock, the formation of Earth's first sandy beaches, and the accumulation of thickening near-shore wedges of sediments. In short, water became the chief architect of Earth's solid surface."

9   *Why We Cooperate*, Page XV: "To an unprecedented degree, homo sapiens are adapted for acting and thinking cooperatively in cultural groups, and indeed all of human's most impressive cognitive achievements – from complex technologies to linguistic and mathematical symbols to intricate social institutions – are the products not of individuals acting alone, but of individuals interacting."

10   "Mysterious species buried their dead and carved symbols 100,000 years before humans," Ashley Strickland, CNN, June 7, 2023

11   *The Rites of Passage*, Page 147: "Mourning...is a transitional period for the survivors, and they enter it through rites of separation and emerge from it through rites of reintegration into society.....During mourning, the living mourners and the deceased constituted a special group, situated between the world of the living and the world of the dead."

12 *Being Mortal, Medicine and What Matters in the End*, Page 126.

13 *A Year To Live, How To Live This Year As If It Were Your Last*, Page 3: "On their deathbed some people look back on their lives and are overwhelmed by a sense of failure. They have a closet full of regrets."

14 *Successful Aging*, Page xxvii: "When you're at the end of your life...the research literature strongly predicts...you'll probably be saying: 'I wish I had spent more time with loved ones,' or "'I wish I had done more to make a difference in the world.' "

15 *The Nature of Prejudice*, Page 23: "There is a common mental device that permits people to hold prejudgments even in the face of much contradictory evidence...contrary evidence is not admitted and allowed to modify the generalization; rather it is perfunctorily acknowledged but excluded."

16 *Lost Connections, Understanding the Real Causes of Depression – and the Unexpected Solutions, Page* 315: "But it turns out we are all still living in a society, even if we pretend we aren't. The longing for connection never goes away."

17 *Being Mortal, Medicine and What Matters in the End*, Page 235: "People seemed to have two different selves – an experiencing self who endures every moment equally and a remembering self who gives almost all the weight of judgment afterward to two single points in time, the worst moment and the last."

18 Paul Rebillot: *The Call to Adventure, Bringing the Hero's Journey to Everyday Life*, Page 9.

19 https://time.com/archive/6869550/science-the-fleeting-flesh/

20 *Journal of Clinical Medicine and Research*, October, 2003: "A Neurologist Looks at Mind and Brain: The Enchanted Loom." https://pmc.ncbi.nlm.nih.gov/articles/PMC1069062/

21 *Successful Aging*, Page 216: "The anticipation of pain lights many of the same neural regions as actual pain."

22 *Why We Remember*, Page 35: "Each time a neural network is trained to learn a fact, connections between simulated neurons in the network are modified."

23 *Successful Aging*, Page 20: "Flexibility – your ability to easily adapt to changes in plans or your environment – decreases steadily in every decade after twenty."

24 *Successful Aging*, Page 144.

25 *Successful Aging*, Page 68: "It's only through interacting with the world that our infant selves learn to separate sensory inputs."

26 *Politics*, Aristotle, Page 8.

27 In *Leviathan*, Part 9, Hobbes states that in our natural condition, before the establishment of states, we lived in "continual fear and danger of violent death, and the life of man [was] solitary, poor, nasty, brutish, and short."

28 *The Future of Democracy*, Page 169: "Lack of interest in the common good has traditionally led to stagnation of ideas and economic progress."

29 According to Black's Law Dictionary, common law is "the body of law derived from judicial decisions, rather than from statutes or constitutions." (Wikipedia)

In England, which has no written constitution, common law dates back to the 1066 Norman Conquest.

30 *Successful Aging*, Page 32: "Our conception of ourselves and who we are is dependent on a continuous thread, a mental narrative of the experiences we've had and the people we've encountered."

31 *Successful Aging*, Page 98: "Your very sense of self is constructed...it is built out of perceptual inputs and is malleable."

32 *Primitive Religion, Its Nature and Origin*, Page 23.

33 *The Rites of Passage*, Page 3: "Transition from group to group and from one social situation to the next are looked on as implicit in the very fact of existence, so that a man's life comes to be made up of a succession of stages with similar ends and beginnings: birth, social puberty, marriage, fatherhood, advancement to a higher class, occupational specialization, and death."

34 *The Rites of Passage*, Pages 65 and 67: "Physiological puberty and "social puberty" [when it is celebrated by a culture] are essentially different and only rarely converge....These are rites of separation from the asexual world."

35 *The Rites of Passage*, Page 116: "Marriage constitutes the most important of the transitions from one social category to another, because for at least one of the spouses it involves a change of family, clan, village or tribe."

36 *Successful Aging*, Page 202: "Older adults in general are better at emotional regulation: they are better able to control their feelings, are less reactive to insults, and pay more attention to the positive things in their lives."

37 https://www.statista.com/statistics/248619/leading-causes-of-death-in-the-us/

38 https://www.news-medical.net/life-sciences/What-Chemical-Elements-are-Found-in-the-Human-Body.aspx

39 From *The Divine Within: Selected Writings on Enlightenment.*

40 *Successful Aging,* Pages 67-68: "During the first six months of life, the infant brain is unable to clearly distinguish the source of sensory inputs; vision, hearing, smell, touch and taste meld into a unitary perceptual representation...It's only through interacting with the world that our infant selves learn to separate these sensory inputs."

41 https://en.wikipedia.org/wiki/Bauhaus

42 *The Structure of Scientific Revolutions*, Page 111, "Paradigm changes do cause scientists to see the world of their research-engagement differently. In so far as their own recourse to that world is through what they see and do, we may want to say that after a revolution scientists are responding to a different world."

43 *Successful Aging,* Page 77: "The prefrontal cortex is also the first cortical region to show wear and tear as we get older....The more we engage this brain region during daily activities, the better we will be able to control our thoughts and think flexibly."

44 *Successful Aging,* Page 155:"The same stress hormones that are essential for survival can have damaging effects on both physical and mental health if they are secreted over a longer period of time..... Exercise, meditation, listening to music, immersing yourself in nature, and sometimes just talking to friends and having social support can help to reduce

stress significantly."

45 *Successful Aging,* Page 179 and 184: "One of the keys to a long health span and long life is social connectedness. Loneliness is associated with early mortality....People can feel lonely even when surrounded by others....Loneliness is a feeling of being detached from meaningful relationships....The kind of care a mother gives to her offspring actually alters the child's physiological responses to stress throughout its lifespan."

46 *The Rites of Passage,* Page 178: "The rite of 'forgiving'... is a preparatory rite whose object is to make the whole group cohesive."

47 Mayo Clinic: Chronic stress puts your health at risk. https://www.mayoclinic.org/healthy-lifestyle/stress-management/in-depth/stress/art-20046037

48 *Successful Aging,* Page xxiv: "Among the chemical changes we see in the aging brain are a tendency toward forgiveness, tolerance, and acceptance.... Older adults can bring a much-needed compassion to a world being rent by impatience, intolerance, and lack of empathy."

49 *A Year To Live, How To Live This Year As If Were Your Last,* Page 3: "In their last year many people feel as if they have a second chance at growth and inner healing....On their deathbed some people look back on their lives and are overwhelmed by a sense of failure. They have a closet full of regrets."

50 *Being Mortal, Medicine and What Matters in the End,* Page 234: "Courage is strength in the face of knowledge of what is to be feared or hoped. Wisdom is prudent strength. At least two types of courage are required in aging and sickness. The first is the courage to confront the reality of morality – the courage to

seek out the truth of what is to be feared and what is to be hoped....But even more daunting is the second kind of courage – the courage to act on the truth we find....One has to decide whether one's fears or one's hopes are what should matter most."

51 "How Hitler Dismantled a Democracy in 53 Days," Timothy W. Ryback, January 8, 2025, The Atlantic. https://www.yahoo.com/news/hitler-dismantled-democracy-53-days-133000255.html?fr=sycsrp_catchall

52 *The Future of Democracy*, Page 184: "Putin ruled under the constitution left to him by Yeltsin, which allowed him to hold up a façade of democracy while maintaining the same degree of arbitrary power as had existed under the Soviets."

53 https://www.theguardian.com/us-news/video/2024/jul/30/donald-trump-vote-claim

54 *Man's Search for Meaning*, Page 86.

55 *Long Walk to Freedom*, Page 624

56 *Long Walk to Freedom*, Page 622

57 *Successful Aging*, Page 191: "Gratitude is an important and often overlooked emotion and state of mind. Gratitude causes us to focus on what's good about our lives rather than what's bad, shifting our outlook toward the positive."

58 *How We Die*, Page 269.

59 *Why We Remember*, Page 44: "Our emotions contribute to context, which means that our feelings in the present affect what we recall from the past."

60 "I Shall Be Released" song by Bob Dylan, 1967.

61 Phiroze Hansotia, *A Neurologist Looks at Mind*

and Brain: "The Enchanted Loom," Journal of Clinical Medicine and Research, October, 2003: "The human brain, the most complex object in the universe, comprises a hundred billion neurons linked in networks that give rise to intelligence, emotion, consciousness, memory and creativity. Emerging from the collective activity of all brain regions is the most fascinating neurological phenomenon of all – the mind."

62 *Successful Aging,* Page 280: "We evolved in a world that required us to explore the environment, to move. Without that stimulation the brain ceases to function at its full potential."

63 *The Good Life,* Page 10: "The Harvard Study of Adult Development, an extraordinary scientific endeavor that began in 1938…is still going strong today…. One crucial factor stands out for the consistency and power of its ties to physical health, mental health, and longevity. Contrary to what many people might think it's not career achievement, or exercise, or a healthy diet. Don't get us wrong: these things matter (a lot). But one thing continually demonstrates its broad and enduring importance: Good relationships keep us healthier and happier."

64 *Successful Aging,* Page 157: "Stressful experience can lead to very different outcomes….Some people develop resilience, grit, tenacity and focus. Others fall apart."

65 *Longevity Hubs,* Page 17: "As Stanford psychologist Carol Dweck's research has demonstrated, a 'growth mindset' – the belief that talents can be developed with practice – positively impacts health and well-being….In some of the most vibrant older populations around the world, healthy living tends to coincide with continuous learning, as well as regular interactions among older and younger generations."

66 *The Body Keeps the Score: Brain Mind and Body in the Healing of Trauma*, Page 75: "We instinctively read the dynamic between two people simply from their tension or relaxation, their postures and tone of voice, their changing facial expressions."

67 "A Blueprint for Intergenerational Housing," by Jennier Molinksy, Director of Harvard's *Housing in an Aging Society Program*. https://www.jchs.harvard.edu/blog/blueprint-intergenerational-living

68 *Longevity Hubs*, Pages 14 and 17.

69 *Lost Connections*, Page 94: "Every human instinct is honed not for life on your own...because humans need tribes as much as bees need a hive."

www.ingramcontent.com/pod-product-compliance
Lightning Source LLC
Chambersburg PA
CBHW060530080526
44586CB00012B/691